SMOKING
FISH AND SEAFOOD

COMPLETE SMOKER COOKBOOK FOR REAL BARBECUE
ULTIMATE HOW-TO GUIDE FOR SMOKED FISH AND SEAFOOD

ADAM JONES

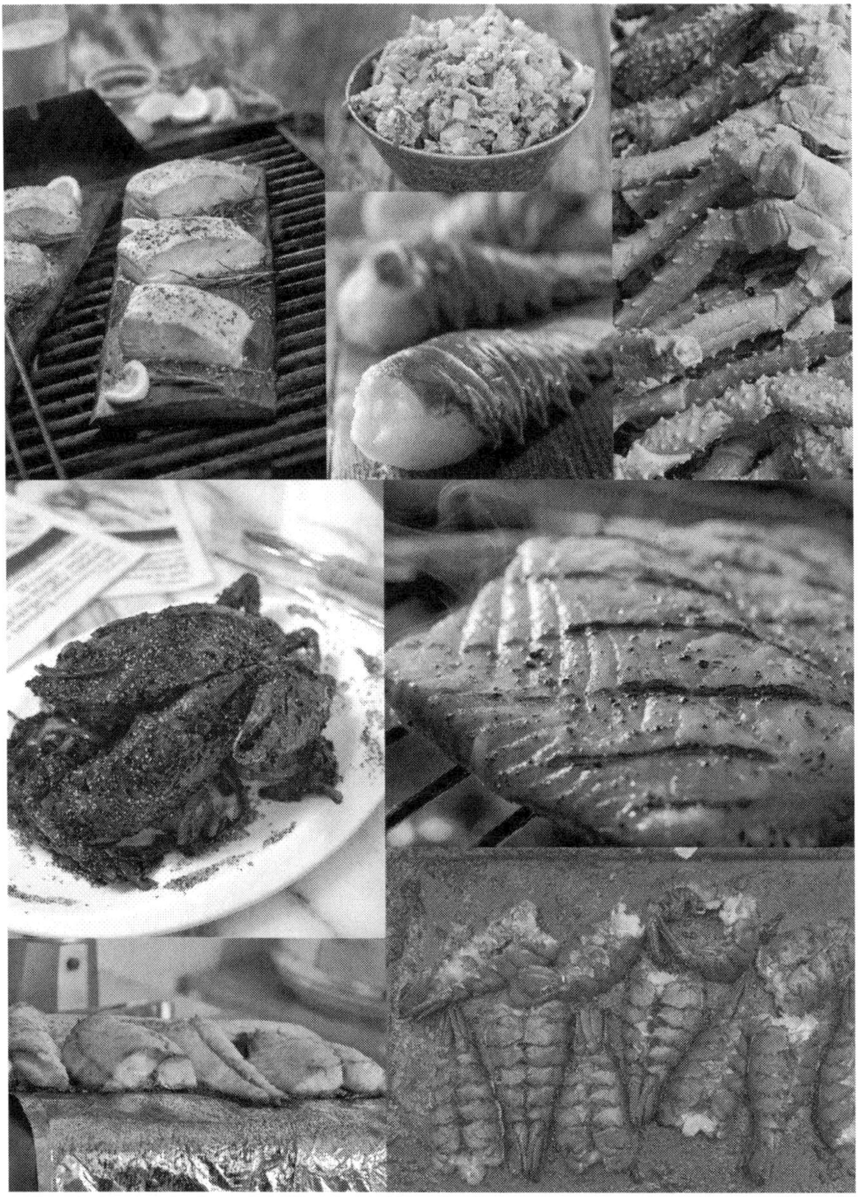

TABLE OF CONTENTS

Information About Smoking Meat.....96

INTRODUCTION

The ultimate how-to guide for smoking all types of fish and seafood. This book on smoking fish for beginners is the guide to mastering the low and slow art of smoking fish and seafood at your home. An essential book for beginners who wants to smoke meat without needing expert help from others. The book offers detailed guidance obtained by years of smoking fish, includes clear instructions and step-by-step directions for every recipe.

This is the only guide you will ever need to professionally smoke a variety of seafood. The book includes full-color photographs of every finished meal to make your job easier. Whether you are a beginner fish smoker or looking to go beyond the basics, the book gives you the tools and tips you need to start that perfectly smoked fish and seafood.

Smoking meat or making BBQ is not only a means of cooking but for some individuals and classy enthusiasts, this is a form of Art! Or dare I say a form of lifestyle! Enthusiasts all around the world have been experimenting and dissecting the secrets of perfectly smoked meat for decades now, and in our golden age, perhaps they have cracked it up completely! In our age, the technique of Barbecuing or Smoking meat has been perfected to such a level, that a BBQ Grill is pretty much an essential amenity found in all backyard or sea-beach parties!

This is the drinking fountain for the more hip and adventurous people, who prefer to have a nice chat with their friends and families while smoking up a few batches of Burger Patty for them to enjoy. But here's the thing, while this art might seem as a very easy form of cooking which only requires you to flip meats over and over! Mastering it might be a little bit difficult if you don't know have the proper information with you. And that is exactly why I have written this chapter, where I will walk you through the very basic elements of Smoking, so that you may start off experimenting with the recipes in no time at all! Let's start with a very basic question, the answer to which should be known to all budding smokers and master pitters out there!

FIND MORE INFORMATION ABOUT SMOKING MEAT AT THE END OF THE BOOK

FISH RECIPES

CINNAMON SWEET BROWN SMOKED SALMON

(TOTAL COOK TIME 3 HOURS 10 MINUTES)

INGREDIENTS FOR 10 SERVINGS

- Salmon fillet (5-lbs., 2.3-kgs)

THE RUB

- Brown sugar – 3 tablespoons

- Cumin – 2 teaspoons

- Salt – 1 teaspoon

- Chopped parsley – 1 teaspoon

- Chili powder – 2 teaspoons

- Garlic powder – 2 tablespoons

- Mustard – ½ teaspoon

- Paprika – ½ teaspoon

- Pepper – ½ teaspoon

- Cinnamon – 1 teaspoon

- Olive oil – 2 tablespoons

THE FIRE

- Preheat the smoker an hour prior to smoking.

- Use pecan wood chips for the smoking.

METHOD

1. Preheat a smoker to 225°F (107°C) and use indirect heat. Don't forget to soak the wood chips before using.

2. Place brown sugar, cumin, salt, chopped parsley, chili powder, garlic powder, mustard, paprika, and pepper in a bowl. Mix well.

3. Rub the salmon with the spice mixture and let it sit.

4. Once the smoker has reached the desired temperature, place the salmon on the smoker's rack and sprinkle cinnamon on top.

5. Smoke the salmon for 3 hours or until opaque.

6. Remove the smoked salmon from the smoker and transfer to a serving dish.

7. Serve and enjoy.

SMOKED SEA BASS WITH BUTTER AND GARLIC

(TOTAL COOK TIME 3 HOURS 10 MINUTES)

INGREDIENTS FOR 10 SERVINGS

- Sea bass fillet (4-lbs., 1.8-kgs)

THE SPICE

- Butter – ½ cup
- Lemon juice – ¼ cup
- Olive oil – 3 tablespoons
- Chopped parsley – 2 tablespoons
- Minced garlic – 3 tablespoons

- Onion powder – ½ teaspoon

- Paprika – ½ teaspoon

- Salt – ½ teaspoon

THE FIRE

- Preheat the smoker an hour prior to smoking.

- Use charcoal and hickory wood chips for the smoking.

METHOD

1. Preheat a smoker to 225°F (107°C). Use the soaked hickory wood chips.

2. Rub the sea bass fillet with minced garlic then set aside.

3. Melt butter and combine with lemon juice and olive oil.

4. Brush butter mixture over the sea bass fillet then sprinkle onion powder, paprika, and salt on top.

5. Place the sea bass on the smoker's rack and smoke for 2 hours. Brush with the butter mixture every 30 minutes.

6. Once the smoked sea bass is ready, remove from the smoker and place in a serving dish.

7. Serve and enjoy.

SMOKED HALIBUT WITH HONEY LEMON GLAZE

(TOTAL COOK TIME 4 HOURS 10 MINUTES)

INGREDIENTS FOR 10 SERVINGS

- Halibut fillet (4-lbs., 1.8-kgs)

THE MARINATE

- Minced garlic – 3 tablespoons
- Olive oil – ½ cup

- Salt – 3 tablespoons

- Black pepper – 3 tablespoons

The Glaze

- Raw honey – ½ cup

- Lemon juice – 3 tablespoons

The Fire

- Preheat the smoker an hour prior to smoking.

- Use pecan wood chips for the smoking.

Method

1. Preheat a smoker to 225°F (107°C). Use the soaked pecan wood chips.

2. Combine minced garlic with salt and pepper then pour olive oil over the spice. Mix well.

3. Rub the halibut with the spice mixture then wrap with aluminum foil.

4. Place the wrapped halibut in the smoker then smoke it for 2 hours.

5. Once it is done, remove from the smoker then let it sit until just a bit warm.

6. Unwrap the halibut and place on a serving dish.

7. Combine honey with lemon then drizzle over the smoked halibut.

8. Serve and enjoy.

Spicy Smoked Salmon with Peanut Oil

(TOTAL COOK TIME 4 HOURS 10 MINUTES)

INGREDIENTS FOR 10 SERVINGS

- Salmon fillet (5-lbs., 2.3-kgs)

THE MARINATE

- Peanut oil – ½ cup

- Soy sauce – ¼ cup

- Balsamic vinegar – ¼ cup

- Chopped onion – ¼ cup

- Chili paste – 3 tablespoons

- Brown sugar – 1 tablespoon

- Minced garlic – 2 teaspoons

- Ginger – 2 teaspoons

- Salt – 1 ½ tablespoons

THE FIRE

- Preheat the smoker an hour prior to smoking.

- Use charcoal and hickory wood chips for the smoking.

METHOD

1. Combine all of the spices in a bowl then mix well.

2. Rub the salmon fillet with the spice mixture then marinate for an hour.

3. Preheat a smoker to 225°F (107°C) and use indirect heat. Don't forget to soak the wood chips before using.

4. Once the smoker is ready, place the marinated salmon on the smoker's rack then smoke for 3 hours. Check the smoke and add more wood chips if it is necessary.

5. When the salmon is done, take it out from the smoker and transfer to a serving dish.

6. Serve and enjoy.

Smoked Tuna Teriyaki

(TOTAL COOK TIME 2 HOURS 10 MINUTES)

INGREDIENTS FOR 10 SERVINGS

- Tuna fillet (4-lbs., 1.8-kgs)

THE MARINATE

- Teriyaki sauce – ½ cup

- Soy sauce – ½ cup

- Pepper – 2 tablespoons

THE TOPPING

- Sesame seeds – ¼ cup

THE FIRE

- Preheat the smoker an hour prior to smoking.

- Use charcoal and hickory wood chips for the smoking.

METHOD

1. Place teriyaki sauce, soy sauce, and pepper in a zipper-lock plastic bag. Stir until incorporated.

2. Add tuna fillet to the plastic bag then seal it properly.

3. Shake the plastic bag until the tuna fillet is completely coated with the seasoning mixture then marinate at least 5 hours or overnight. Store in the refrigerator to keep it fresh.

4. Preheat a smoker to 225°F (107°C). Use the soaked hickory wood chips.

5. Meanwhile, take the plastic bag out from the refrigerator then thaw it for a few minutes.

6. Transfer the seasoned tuna to a disposable aluminum pan together with the liquid then place in the smoker.

7. Smoke the tuna for 2 hours then take it out from the smoker.

8. Transfer to a serving dish then serve.

SMOKED SWORDFISH WITH GINGER AND LIME

(TOTAL COOK TIME 3 HOURS 10 MINUTES)

INGREDIENTS FOR 10 SERVINGS

- Swordfish fillet (4-lbs., 1.8-kgs)

THE MARINADE

- Honey – ½ cup
- Soy sauce – ½ cup

- Olive oil – ¼ cup

- Minced garlic – 3 tablespoons

- Ginger – 2 teaspoons

- Lime zest – 1 teaspoon

- Pepper – 1 teaspoon

THE FIRE

- Preheat the smoker an hour prior to smoking.

- Use charcoal and hickory wood chips for the smoking.

METHOD

1. Combine honey, soy sauce, olive oil, minced garlic, ginger, lime zest, and pepper in a bowl. Mix well.

2. Rub the swordfish fillet with the spice mixture and marinate for an hour. Place in a disposable aluminum pan.

3. Preheat a smoker to 225°F (107°C). Use the soaked hickory wood chips.

4. Once the smoker is ready, place aluminum pan in the smoker.

5. Smoke the swordfish for 2 hours. Flip the swordfish fillet after an hour.

6. Once it is done, remove from the smoker and place on a serving dish.

7. Serve and enjoy.

Smoked Catfish with Special Herbs

(TOTAL COOK TIME 4 HOURS 10 MINUTES)

INGREDIENTS FOR 10 SERVINGS

- Catfish fillet (4-lbs., 1.8-kgs)

THE MARINADE

- Olive oil – 1 ½ cups
- Red wine vinegar – ¾ cup
- Lemon juice – 3 tablespoons
- Minced garlic – 2 tablespoons
- Oregano – 3 tablespoons
- Thyme – 1 ½ tablespoons

- Basil – 1 ½ tablespoons

- Black pepper – 2 teaspoons

- Cayenne pepper – 1 ½ teaspoons

- Salt – 2 tablespoons

- Sugar – ¼ cup

THE FIRE

- Preheat the smoker an hour prior to smoking.

- Use charcoal and hickory wood chips for the smoking.

METHOD

1. Combine all of the marinade ingredients in a container then mix well.

2. Marinate the catfish in the spice mixture for at least an hour. It is better to store it in the refrigerator to keep it fresh.

3. Preheat a smoker to 225°F (107°C).

4. When the smoker has reached the desired temperature, remove the marinated catfish from the refrigerator and place on the smoker's rack.

5. Smoke the catfish for 3 hours and once it is done, take the smoked catfish out from the smoker then transfer to a serving dish.

6. Serve and enjoy.

Lemon Soy Smoked Trout

(TOTAL COOK TIME 5 HOURS 10 MINUTES)

INGREDIENTS FOR 10 SERVINGS

- Trout (5-lbs., 2.3-kgs)

THE MARINATE

- Lemon juice – 1 cup

- Soy sauce – 1 cup

- Salt – ½ cup

- Cayenne pepper – ¼ cup

- Black pepper – ¼ cup

The Topping

- Fresh lemons - 5

The Fire

- Preheat the smoker an hour prior to smoking.

- Use charcoal and hickory wood chips for the smoking.

Method

1. Combine salt with black pepper and cayenne pepper then mix well.

2. Pour lemon juice and soy sauce into the mixture then stir to combine.

3. Rub the trout with the spice mixture then marinate 2 hours.

4. Fill the smoker's hopper with soaked hickory wood chips then preheat to 225°F (107°C).

5. Once the smoker has reached the desired temperature, place the marinated trout on the smoker's rack.

6. Cut the fresh lemons into slices then arrange them on the top of the trout. Smoke the trout for 3 hours.

7. Once it is done, take the smoked trout from the smoker.

8. Serve.

Smoked Tuna Salads

(TOTAL COOK TIME 4 HOURS 20 MINUTES)

INGREDIENTS FOR 10 SERVINGS

- Tuna fillet (2-lbs., 0,9-kgs)

THE SPICE

- Olive oil – 3 tablespoons

- Salt – 2 tablespoons

- Pepper – 1 tablespoon

THE ADDITIONAL INGREDIENTS

- Mayonnaise – ¾ cup

- Chopped onion – ½ cup

- Chopped leek – ½ cup

- Lemon juice – 1 tablespoon

THE FIRE

- Preheat the smoker an hour prior to smoking.

- Add charcoal and bagel chips during the smoking time.

METHOD

1. Preheat a smoker to 225°F (107°C). Don't forget to soak the wood chips before using.

2. Brush the tuna fillet with olive oil then sprinkle salt and pepper over the tuna fillet. Let it sit until the smoker is ready.

3. Once the smoker has reached the desired temperature, place the seasoned tuna fillet on the smoker's rack.

4. Smoke for 4 hours until tender.

5. Take the smoked tuna out from the smoker then place on a flat surface.

6. Using a fork shred the smoked tuna then place in a salad bowl.

7. Add mayonnaise, chopped onion, and chopped leek to the salad bowl then splash lemon juice on top. Toss to combine.

8. Serve and enjoy immediately.

Spicy Brown Smoked Catfish

(TOTAL COOK TIME 7 HOURS 10 MINUTES)

INGREDIENTS FOR 10 SERVINGS

- Whole Catfish (4-lbs., 1.8-kgs)

THE MARINATE

- Water

- Salt – ¾ cup

- Brown sugar – 1 ¼ cups

- Soy sauce – ¾ cup

- Minced garlic – 3 tablespoons

- Black pepper – 1 ½ teaspoons

- Cayenne pepper – 1 ½ teaspoons

THE FIRE

- Preheat the smoker an hour prior to smoking.

- Add apple wood chips for the smoking.

METHOD

1. Combine salt, brown sugar, soy sauce, minced garlic, black pepper, and cayenne pepper in a container.

2. Pour water into the container then mix until the spices are completely dissolved.

3. Stir in catfish to the container and marinate for at least 4 hours. Store in the refrigerator to keep it fresh.

4. Preheat a smoker to 225°F (107°C).

5. When the smoker is ready, remove the catfish from the refrigerator and place on the smoker's rack.

6. Smoke the catfish fillet for 3 hours.

7. Once it is done, remove from the smoker and transfer to a serving dish.

8. Enjoy.

Smoked Whole Mackerel with Thyme

(total cook time 4 Hours 20 minutes)

Ingredients for 10 servings

- Whole Mackerel (2,5-lbs., 1.1-kgs)

The Spice

- Olive oil – ¼ cup

- Salt – 2 tablespoons

- Thyme – 5 sprigs

The Fire

- Preheat the smoker an hour prior to smoking.

- Add alder wood chips during the smoking time.

Method

1. Rub the mackerels with salt and olive oil then place thyme in the cavity. Set aside.

2. Preheat a smoker to 225°F (107°C).

3. Once the smoker has reached the desired temperature, place the mackerels on the smoker's rack then smoke for 4 hours.

4. Check the smoke and add more wood chips if it is necessary.

5. When the smoked mackerels are ready, take it out from the smoker then place on a serving dish.

6. Serve with salads, pasta, or dip, as you desired.

Aromatic Smoked Fish with Lemongrass

(TOTAL COOK TIME 4 HOURS 20 MINUTES)

INGREDIENTS FOR 10 SERVINGS

- Fresh fillet (4-lbs., 1.8-kgs)

THE SPICE

- Ginger – 3 tablespoons

- Red chili flakes – 3 tablespoons

- Lemongrass – 10

- Soy sauce – 3 tablespoons

- Lemon juice – 3 tablespoons

- Sliced shallot – 3 tablespoons

- Pepper – 1 teaspoon

The Additional Ingredients

- Banana leaves

The Fire

- Preheat the smoker an hour prior to smoking.

- Add charcoal and bagel chips during the smoking time.

Method

1. Preheat a smoker to 225°F (107°C). Don't forget to soak the wood chips before using.

2. Cut the lemongrass into slices then place in a bowl.

3. Add pepper and ginger to the mixture then mix well.

4. Rub the fish with lemon juice and soy sauce then place on the banana leaves.

5. Sprinkle lemongrass mixture over the fish and wrap with banana leaves. Secure with toothpicks.

6. Place the wrapped fish on the smoker's rack then smoke the fish for 4 hours.

7. Once it is done, remove from the smoker then let it sit for a few minutes.

8. Unwrap the fish then transfer to a serving dish.

9. Serve and enjoy.

Hot and Sweet Smoked Mackerel

(Total cook time 3 Hours 10 minutes)

Ingredients for 10 servings

- Mackerel (3 lbs., 1.4-kgs)

The Marinate

- Salt – 6 tablespoons

- Sugar – 6 tablespoons

- Black pepper – 3 tablespoons

- Dijon mustard – 1 ½ tablespoons

- Lemon juice – 4 tablespoons

The Fire

- Preheat the smoker an hour prior to smoking.

- Add charcoal and hardwood chips for the smoking.

Method

1. Combine salt with sugar, black pepper, Dijon mustard, and lemon juice in a bowl. Mix well.

2. Rub the mackerel with the spice mixture then marinate for at least an hour.

3. Heat up the smoker to 225°F (107°C).

4. When the smoker is ready, place the seasoned mackerel on the smoker's rack then smoke for at least 2 hours.

5. Check the doneness of the smoked mackerel. Prick a fork on the smoked mackerel and see whether the smoked mackerel is already firm and opaque or not.

6. Once it is done, remove from the smoker and transfer to a serving dish.

7. Serve and enjoy.

Smoked Catfish with Hot Sauce

(TOTAL COOK TIME 11 HOURS 5 MINUTES)

INGREDIENTS FOR 10 SERVINGS

- Catfish fillet (2,5-lbs., 1.1-kgs)

THE BRINE

- Salt – 1 cup

- Water - as needed

THE SPICE

- Hot sauce – 1 ½ cups

- Black pepper – 2 tablespoons

The Fire

- Preheat the smoker an hour prior to smoking.

- Add cherry wood chips during the smoking time.

Method

1. Pour water into a container then add salt to it. Stir until the salt is completely dissolved.

2. Brine the catfish in the salty water overnight then and store in the refrigerator to keep it fresh.

3. In the morning, remove the catfish from the brine then set aside.

4. Preheat a smoker to 225°F (107°C).

5. Once the smoker has reached the desired temperature, place the catfish on the smoker rack then sprinkle black pepper and drizzle hot sauce over the catfish.

6. Smoke the catfish for 3 hours and once it is done, take the smoked catfish out from the smoker.

7. Place the smoked catfish on a serving dish then serve.

SMOKED SALMON SALADS BLACK PEPPER

(TOTAL COOK TIME 4 HOURS 5 MINUTES)

INGREDIENTS FOR 10 SERVINGS

- Salmon fillet (4-lbs., 1.8-kgs)

THE SPICE

- Salt – 3 tablespoons
- Black pepper – ¼ cup
- Olive oil – ¼ cup

THE COMPLEMENT

- Chopped fresh lettuce
- Grated cheese

- Salads dressing, as you desired

- Lemon juice

THE FIRE

- Preheat the smoker an hour prior to smoking.

- Add charcoal and pecan wood chips during the smoking time.

METHOD

1. Preheat a smoker to 225°F (107°C).

2. Meanwhile, brush the salmon fillet with olive oil then sprinkle salt and black pepper over the salmon.

3. Once the smoker has reached the desired temperature, place the salmon on the smoker's rack.

4. Smoke the salmon for 4 hours or until the salmon reaches the desired doneness. Sprinkle salt and black pepper once every hour.

5. When the salmon is done, remove from the smoker and place on a salad dish.

6. Serve with the complement and enjoy right away.

Sweet Brown Smoked Trout on Cedar Plank

(TOTAL COOK TIME 16 HOURS 10 MINUTES)

INGREDIENTS FOR 10 SERVINGS

- Trout (5-lbs., 2.3-kgs)

THE RUB

- Olive oil – ½ cup

- Lemon juice – ½ cup

- Salt – ¼ cup

- Minced garlic – 3 tablespoons

- Brown sugar – ½ cup

The Topping

- Fresh lemons - 5

The Fire

- Preheat the smoker an hour prior to smoking.

- Use charcoal and hickory wood chips for the smoking.

Method

1. Combine salt, minced garlic, brown sugar, olive oil, and lemon juice in a container with a lid.

2. Rub the trout with the spice mixture then marinate overnight. Store in the refrigerator to keep it fresh.

3. In the morning, remove the trout from the refrigerator and thaw until it reaches the room temperature.

4. Preheat a smoker to 225°F (107°C) and wait until it reaches the desired temperature.

5. Place the trout on a cedar plank then lay on the smoker's grates.

6. Smoke the trout for 4 hours and once it is done, remove from the smoker.

7. Serve.

Smoked Salmon Dip

(TOTAL COOK TIME 4 HOURS 20 MINUTES)

INGREDIENTS FOR 10 SERVINGS
- Salmon fillet (2-lbs., 0,9-kgs)

THE SPICE
- Salt – 2 tablespoons
- Minced garlic – ¼ cup

THE ADDITIONAL INGREDIENTS
- Cream cheese 1 cup
- Sour cream 1 cup
- Lemon juice – 2 ½ tablespoons
- Chopped parsley – 1 tablespoon
- Black pepper – ¾ teaspoon

THE FIRE

- Preheat the smoker an hour prior to smoking.

- Add charcoal and bagel chips during the smoking time.

METHOD

1. Preheat a smoker to 225°F (107°C). Don't forget to soak the wood chips before using.

2. Rub the salmon fillet with salt and minced garlic let it sit for about 30minutes.

3. When the smoker is ready, place the seasoned salmon fillet in the smoker.

4. Smoke the salmon fillet for 4 hours until tender.

5. Remove the smoked salmon from the smoker then place on a flat surface.

6. Divide the smoked salmon into halves.

7. Cut half of the smoked salmon into small cubes then place in a food processor.

8. Add cream cheese, sour cream, lemon juice, chopped parsley and black pepper then pulse until smooth.

9. Transfer to a container with a lid then set aside.

10. Using a fork shred the other half smoked salmon then add to the container. Mix well.

11. Enjoy the salmon dip with bagel, chips, or crackers.

TRADITIONAL SMOKED TILAPIA

(TOTAL COOK TIME 16 HOURS 10 MINUTES)

INGREDIENTS FOR 10 SERVINGS

- Fresh Tilapia (5-lbs., 2.3-kgs)

THE RUB

- Minced garlic – ½ cup

- Coriander – ¼ cup

- Salt – 2 tablespoons

THE GLAZE

- Olive oil – ¼ cup

The Fire

- Preheat the smoker an hour prior to smoking.

- Use charcoal and hickory wood chips for the smoking.

Method

1. Rub the fish with salt, coriander, and minced garlic then let it sit overnight.

2. Store the fish in the refrigerator to keep it fresh.

3. In the morning, remove the tilapia from the refrigerator and thaw until it reaches the room temperature.

4. Preheat a smoker to 225°F (107°C) and wait until it reaches the desired temperature.

5. Brush the seasoned tilapia with olive oil then place it on a smoker's rack.

6. Smoke the tilapia for 4 hours and once it is done, remove from the smoker.

7. Serve.

ORIGINAL TUNA LEMON

(TOTAL COOK TIME 3 HOURS 5 MINUTES)

INGREDIENTS FOR 10 SERVINGS

- Tuna fillet (4-lbs., 1.8-kgs)

THE SPICE

- Salt – 3 tablespoons

- Olive oil – 3 tablespoons

- Fresh lemons - 5

THE FIRE

- Preheat the smoker an hour prior to smoking.

- Add charcoal and apple wood chips during the smoking time.

METHOD

1. Preheat a smoker to 225°F (107°C).

2. Brush the tuna fillet with olive oil then sprinkle salt over the tuna.

3. Cut the fresh lemons into slices then arrange half of them on a sheet of aluminum foil.

4. Place the tuna fillet on the lemon slices then arrange the remaining lemon slices on top.

5. Wrap the tuna with aluminum foil then place in the smoker.

6. Smoke the tuna for 3 hours then take it out from the smoker.

7. Unwrap the tuna fillet then transfer to a serving dish.

8. Enjoy!

Smoked Haddock with White Sauce

(TOTAL COOK TIME 3 HOURS 10 MINUTES)

INGREDIENTS FOR 10 SERVINGS

- Haddock fillet (4-lbs., 1.8-kgs)

THE RUB

- Lemon juice – ¼ cup

- Minced garlic – 3 tablespoons

- Salt – 3 tablespoons

- Pepper – 2 tablespoons

The Sauce

- Fresh milk – 3 cups

- Chopped onion – ½ cup

- Butter – 3 tablespoons

- Plain flour – 2 tablespoons

- Chopped parsley – 2 tablespoons

The Fire

- Preheat the smoker an hour prior to smoking.

- Use charcoal and hickory wood chips for the smoking.

Method

1. Preheat a smoker to 225°F (107°C). Use indirect heat and don't forget to soak the wood chips before using.

2. Combine minced garlic with lemon juice, salt, and pepper then mix well.

3. Rub the haddock fillet with the spice mixture then wrap with aluminum foil.

4. When the smoker is ready, place the wrapped haddock fillet on the smoker's rack then smoke for 3 hours.

5. Meanwhile, preheat a saucepan over medium heat then melt butter in it.

6. Stir in chopped onion then sauté until translucent and aromatic.

7. Pour about 2 cups of milk over the saucepan then bring to boil.

8. Combine flour with the remaining milk then stir until incorporated.

9. Once the sauce is boiled, pour the flour and milk mixture into the saucepan then stir until thickened.

10. Stir in chopped parsley then remove from heat.

11. When the smoked haddock is done, remove from the smoker and let it sit for a few minutes.

12. Unwrap the smoked haddock then place on a serving dish.

13. Drizzle the sauce over the smoked haddock then serve.

14. Enjoy!

SMOKED TILAPIA FILLET WITH HERBS

(TOTAL COOK TIME 3 HOURS 10 MINUTES)

INGREDIENTS FOR 10 SERVINGS

- Tilapia fillet (4-lbs., 1.8-kgs)

THE RUB

- Basil – ¼ cup
- Bay leaves – 3
- Marjoram – 3 tablespoons
- Salt – 3 tablespoons
- Garlic powder – 3 tablespoons
- Pepper – 2 tablespoons

THE FIRE

- Preheat the smoker an hour prior to smoking.

- Use apple wood chips for the smoking.

METHOD

1. Preheat a smoker to 225°F (107°C). Use indirect heat and don't forget to soak the wood chips before using.

2. Rub the tilapia fillet with basil, marjoram, salt, garlic powder, and pepper then place on a sheet of aluminum foil.

3. Place bay leaves on top then wrap the tilapia aluminum foil.

4. Once the smoker has reached the desired temperature, place the wrapped tilapia in the smoker.

5. Smoked the tilapia for 3 hours and once it is done, remove the smoked tilapia from the smoker and let it warm for a few minutes.

6. Unwrap the smoked the tilapia and place on a serving dish.

7. Serve and enjoy.

TASTY SMOKED KINGFISH IN MAPLE AROMA

(TOTAL COOK TIME 3 HOURS 10 MINUTES)

INGREDIENTS FOR 10 SERVINGS

- Kingfish fillet (4-lbs., 1.8-kgs)

THE MARINATE

- Maple syrup – 1 cup

THE FIRE

- Preheat the smoker an hour prior to smoking.

- Use apple wood chips for the smoking.

METHOD

1. Rub the kingfish fillet with maple syrup then marinate overnight. Store in the refrigerator to keep the kingfish fillet fresh.

2. In the morning, take the kingfish fillet out from the refrigerator then thaw until it reaches the room temperature.

3. Preheat a smoker to 225°F (107°C). Use indirect heat and don't forget to soak the wood chips before using.

4. Once the smoker is ready, place the seasoned kingfish fillet on the smoker's rack and smoke for 3 hours.

5. When the smoked kingfish is done, remove from the smoker then transfer to a serving dish.

6. Serve and enjoy.

Smoked Gingery Halibut

(TOTAL COOK TIME 3 HOURS 10 MINUTES)

INGREDIENTS FOR 10 SERVINGS

- Halibut fillet (5-lbs., 2.3-kgs)

THE RUB

- Lemon juice – 3 tablespoons
- Ginger – 1 tablespoon
- Salt – 1 ½ tablespoons
- Coriander – 2 tablespoons

THE FIRE

- Preheat the smoker an hour prior to smoking.
- Use pecan wood chips for the smoking.

METHOD

1. Season the halibut with lemon juice; ginger, salt, and coriander then warp with aluminum foil.

2. Let the halibut sit for about an hour while waiting for the smoker.

3. Preheat a smoker to 225°F (107°C) and use indirect heat. Don't forget to soak the wood chips before using.

4. When the smoker is ready, place the wrapped halibut in the smoker.

5. Smoke the halibut for 4 hours and once it is done, remove the smoked halibut from the smoker.

6. Unwrap the smoked halibut and place on a serving dish.

7. Serve and enjoy.

Refreshing Smoked Kingfish with Pineapple Salads

(total cook time 3 Hours 10 minutes)

Ingredients for 10 servings

- Kingfish fillet (4-lbs., 1.8-kgs)

The Rub

- Lemon juice – 3 tablespoons
- Chili powder – 1 ½ teaspoons
- Salt – 2 teaspoons
- Pepper – 1 teaspoon

The Salads

- Fresh pineapples – 3

- Diced tomato – 2 cups

- Lemon juice – 3 tablespoons

The Fire

- Preheat the smoker an hour prior to smoking.

- Use apple wood chips for the smoking.

Method

1. Season the Kingfish fillet with salt, pepper, chili powder, and lemon juice then let it sit for about an hour.

2. Preheat a smoker to 225°F (107°C). Use indirect heat and don't forget to soak the wood chips before using.

3. Meanwhile, peel the pineapple then cut into slices.

4. When the smoker is ready, place the seasoned kingfish on the smoker's rack then top with pineapple slices.

5. Smoke the kingfish for 3 hours and once it is done transfer to a serving dish.

6. Place the smoked pineapple slices on a flat surface then cut into small cubes.

7. Combine the pineapple cubes with diced tomato then drizzle lemon juice on top. Toss to combine.

8. Top the smoked kingfish with pineapple salads then serve and enjoy.

SPICY SMOKED FISH FILLET WITH CLOVE AROMA

(TOTAL COOK TIME 12 HOURS 10 MINUTES)

Ingredients for 10 servings

- Snapper (4-lbs., 1.8-kgs)

The Marinade

- Soy sauce – ½ cup

- Oyster sauce – ¼ cup

- Fish sauce – 2 ½ tablespoons

- Brown sugar – ¼ cup

- Cloves – 10

- Lemon juice – 2 tablespoons

The Fire

- Preheat the smoker an hour prior to smoking.

- Use pecan wood chips for the smoking.

Method

1. Place soy sauce, oyster sauce, fish sauce, brown sugar, and lemon juice in a zipper-lock plastic bag. Mix well.

2. Put the snappers in the plastic bag then seal it properly. Shake until the snappers are completely coated with the seasoning mixture.

3. Marinate the snappers overnight or at least 4 hours. Store in the refrigerator to keep it fresh.

4. In the morning, preheat a smoker to 225°F (107°C).

5. Remove the snappers from the refrigerator then take them out from the plastic bag.

6. When the smoker is ready, place the snappers on the smoker's rack. Give space between each snapper.

7. Smoke the snappers for 4 hours. Don't forget to add wood chips to the smoker if it is needed.

8. Once it is done, remove the smoked snappers from the smoker and transfer to a serving dish.

9. Serve and enjoy.

SEAFOOD RECIPES

BUTTERY SMOKED CRAB LEGS WITH LEMON

(TOTAL COOK TIME 30 MINUTES)

Ingredients for 10 servings

- King Crab Legs – 5 (5-lbs., 2.3-kgs)

The Spice

- Butter – 1 ¼ cups

- Lemon juice – ¼ cup

- Pepper – 2 tablespoons

- Lemon zest – ½ teaspoon

- Garlic powder – 2 tablespoons

The Fire

- Preheat the smoker an hour prior to smoking.

- Add charcoal and hickory chips during the smoking time.

Method

1. Place butter in a microwave-safe bowl then microwave until melted.

2. Add pepper, lemon, zest, and garlic powder to the melted butter then pour lemon juice into the bowl. Stir well.

3. Place the crab legs in a disposable aluminum pan then brush with the butter mixture.

4. Preheat a smoker to 225°F (107°C) and use indirect heat.

5. Once the smoker is ready, place the disposable aluminum pan with crab legs in the smoker.

6. Smoke the crab legs for 30 minutes and brush with the remaining butter mixture every 10 minutes.

7. When the smoked crab legs are done, remove from the smoker and transfer to a serving dish.

8. Enjoy right away.

SMOKED SPICY SQUIDS WITH SOY SAUCE

(TOTAL COOK TIME 1 HOUR 30 MINUTES)

INGREDIENTS FOR 10 SERVINGS

- Fresh Squids (3-lbs., 1.4-kgs)

THE BRINE

- Water – 1 gallon

- Salt – 1 ¼ cups

- Sugar – 1 ¼ cups

- Soy sauce – 1 ¼ cups

- Lemon zest – 2 teaspoons

- Lemon juice – ½ cup

THE FIRE

- Preheat the smoker an hour prior to smoking.

- Add charcoal and hickory chips during the smoking time.

METHOD

1. Combine sugar, salt, and lemon zest in a container then pour water into it.

2. Add soy sauce and lemon juice to the brine then mix well.

3. Stir in the squids to the container and brine them for an hour.

4. Add soaked hickory chips to the smoker's hopper then preheat the smoker to 225°F (107°C).

5. When the smoker is ready, take the squids out from the brine then place on the smoker's rack.

6. Smoke the squids for 30 minutes and remove from the smoker.

7. Arrange the smoked squids on a serving dish then cut into slices if it is necessary.

8. Serve with lemon slices and enjoy.

Smoked Lobster Tails Garlic

(TOTAL COOK TIME 50 MINUTES)

INGREDIENTS FOR 10 SERVINGS

- Lobster Tails – 10 (5-lbs., 2.3-kgs)

THE SPICE

- Butter – 1 cup

- Minced garlic – ¼ cup

- Pepper – 2 teaspoons

THE FIRE

- Preheat the smoker an hour prior to smoking.

- Add charcoal and hickory chips during the smoking time.

METHOD

1. Add soaked hickory chips to the smoker's hopper then preheat the smoker to 225°F (107°C).

2. Place the lobster tails in a disposable aluminum pan then set aside.

3. Preheat a saucepan over medium heat then place butter in it.

4. Once the butter is melted, stir in minced garlic then sauté until aromatic. Remove from heat.

5. Add pepper to the saucepan then stir well.

6. Pour the butter mixture over the lobster tails then toss to combine.

7. When the smoker is ready, place the disposable aluminum pan with lobster tails in the smoker.

8. Smoke the lobster tails for 45 minutes and once it is done, remove from the smoker and transfer to a serving dish.

9. Serve and enjoy warm.

SMOKED SCALLOPS IN BACON BLANKETS

(TOTAL COOK TIME 30 MINUTES)

INGREDIENTS FOR 10 SERVINGS

- Jumbo Scallops (5-lbs., 2.3-kgs)
- Bacon – 10 slices

THE SPICE

- Butter – 1 cup
- Salt – 1 teaspoon
- Pepper – 2 tablespoons

The Fire

- Preheat the smoker an hour prior to smoking.

- Add charcoal and hickory chips during the smoking time.

Method

1. Wrap each scallop with bacon then prick using a toothpick.

2. Arrange in a disposable aluminum pan then set aside.

3. Preheat a saucepan over medium heat then melt butter in it. Remove from heat.

4. Add pepper and salt to the melted butter then mix well.

5. Pour the melted butter with spices over the scallops then set aside.

6. Preheat a smoker to 225°F (107°C).

7. When the smoker is ready, place the aluminum pan with scallops in the smoker and smoke for 30 minutes.

8. Once it is done, remove the smoked scallops from the smoker and transfer to a serving dish.

9. Serve and enjoy warm.

Smoked Shrimps Satay

(TOTAL COOK TIME 35 MINUTES)

INGREDIENTS FOR 10 SERVINGS

- Jumbo Shrimps 40 (3-lbs., 1.4-kgs)

THE RUB

- Olive oil – ¾ cup
- Minced garlic – 3 tablespoons
- Chopped parsley – 3 tablespoons
- Cayenne pepper – 1 teaspoon
- Black pepper – ¾ teaspoon
- Salt -3/4 teaspoon

THE FIRE

- Preheat the smoker an hour prior to smoking.
- Use charcoal and hickory chips for smoking.

METHOD

1. Preheat the smoker to 225°F (107°C).

2. Place olive oil in a bowl then add minced garlic, chopped parsley, cayenne pepper, black pepper, and salt. Mix well.

3. Rub the shrimps with the spice mixture then using skewers prick the shrimps.

4. Once the smoker is ready, place the shrimps on the smoker's rack and smoke for 35 minutes or until the shrimps change to an opaque white color.

5. Transfer the smoked shrimps to a serving dish then enjoy warm.

Tasty Spicy Smoked Squids

(TOTAL COOK TIME 1 HOUR)

INGREDIENTS FOR 10 SERVINGS

- Fresh Squids (3-lbs., 1.4-kgs)

THE RUB

- Smoked paprika – 1 tablespoon

- Cumin – 2 ½ teaspoons

- Salt – 1 teaspoon

- Black pepper – 1 ½ teaspoons

- Cayenne pepper – 1 teaspoon

- Minced garlic – 2 teaspoons

- Lemon juice – 2 tablespoons

- Olive oil – ¼ cup

THE FIRE

- Preheat the smoker an hour prior to smoking.

- Add charcoal and hickory chips during the smoking time.

METHOD

1. Preheat a smoker to 225°F (107°C).

2. Combine all of the rub ingredients in a bowl then mix well.

3. Rub the squids with the spice mixture and marinate for 30 minutes.

4. After 30 minutes, prick the squids with skewers then place them on the smoker's rack.

5. Smoke the squids for 30 minutes and once it is done, remove from the smoker.

6. Arrange the smoked squids on a serving dish then enjoy warm.

Juicy Smoked Clams with Spanish Paprika

(Total cook time 30 Minutes)

Ingredients for 10 servings

- Fresh Clams (5-lbs., 2.3-kgs)

The Rub

- Butter – ½ cup

- Minced garlic – 2 tablespoons

- Spanish paprika – ¼ cup

- Chili powder – 1 tablespoon

- Black pepper – 2 teaspoons

- Beer – 2 cups

- Clam juice – 1 cup

THE FIRE

- Preheat the smoker an hour prior to smoking.

- Add charcoal and hickory chips during the smoking time.

METHOD

1. Preheat a smoker to 225°F (107°C).

2. Place the clams in a disposable aluminum pan then set aside.

3. Preheat a saucepan over medium heat then melt butter in it.

4. Stir in minced garlic then sauté until wilted and aromatic.

5. Put Spanish paprika, chili powder, and black pepper to the saucepan then mix well.

6. Combine with beer and clam juice then pour over the clams.

7. Place the disposable pan in the smoker then smoke for 30 minutes.

8. Once it is done, remove from the smoker and transfer to a serving dish.

9. Serve and enjoy.

CHEESY SMOKED SHRIMPS IN BACON ROLL

(TOTAL COOK TIME 35 MINUTES)

INGREDIENTS FOR 10 SERVINGS

- Jumbo Shrimps 40 (3-lbs., 1.4-kgs)
- Bacon- as needed

THE RUB

- Paprika – 1 tablespoons
- Cayenne pepper – ¾ teaspoon
- Black pepper – ¾ teaspoon
- Salt – ¾ teaspoon

THE FILLING

- Softened cream cheese – 1 cup

- Bread crumbs – 1 cup

THE FIRE

- Preheat the smoker an hour prior to smoking.

- Use charcoal and hickory chips for smoking.

METHOD

1. Preheat the smoker to 225°F (107°C).

2. Peel the fresh shrimps then rub with paprika, cayenne pepper, black pepper, and salt. Let it sit for a few minutes.

3. Cut the bacon into slices then also set aside.

4. Combine softened cream cheese with breadcrumbs then mix well.

5. Lay a slice of bacon the put a fresh shrimp on it. Add cheese and bread crumbs mixture on top then roll the bacon to cover the shrimps. Place in a disposable aluminum pan then repeat with the remaining ingredients.

6. When the smoker has reached the desired temperature, place the disposable aluminum pan in the smoker and smoke for 35 minutes.

7. Check the doneness of the bacon. If you find that the bacon is not tender enough, you can add more smoking time to 10-15 minutes.

8. Once it is done, take the aluminum pan out from the smoker and transfer to a serving dish.

9. Serve and enjoy.

Savory Smoked Crab Legs

(TOTAL COOK TIME 30 MINUTES)

INGREDIENTS FOR 10 SERVINGS

- King Crab Legs – 5 (5-lbs., 2.3-kgs)

THE SPICE

- Butter – 1 cup

- BBQ Rub – 1 tablespoon

- Chopped parsley – 1 tablespoon

- Crab boil seasoning – 1 teaspoon

The Garnish

- Lemon slices – 1 cup

- Cocktail sauce – ½ cup

The Fire

- Preheat the smoker an hour prior to smoking.

- Add charcoal and hickory chips during the smoking time.

Method

1. Preheat a smoker to 225°F (107°C) and use indirect heat.

2. Melt butter then combine with BBQ rubs and crab boil seasoning. Mix well.

3. Brush the crab legs with the spice mixture then place in a disposable aluminum pan.

4. Sprinkle chopped parsley over the crab legs then set aside.

5. When the smoker has reached the desired temperature, place the disposable aluminum pan with crab legs in the smoker.

6. Smoke the crab legs for 30 minutes and once it is done, remove the smoked crab legs from the smoker then transfer to a serving dish.

7. Top with lemon slices and cocktail sauce then serve.

8. Enjoy!

Smoked Shrimps Garlic with Apple Sauce

(TOTAL COOK TIME 1 HOUR 35 MINUTES)

INGREDIENTS FOR 10 SERVINGS

- Fresh Shrimps (5-lbs., 2.3-kgs)

THE RUB

- Olive oil – ½ cup
- Chopped parsley – ½ cup
- Dry sherry – ½ cup
- Lemon zest – 1 tablespoon
- Minced garlic – ¼ cup

- Salt – 2 tablespoons

The Sauce

- Apple juice – 2 cups

- Ketchup – 2 cups

- Mustard – ¼ cup

- Worcestershire sauce – 1 tablespoon

- Brown sugar – ¼ cup

- Smoked paprika – 2 teaspoons

The Fire

- Preheat the smoker an hour prior to smoking.

- Use charcoal and hickory chips for smoking.

Method

1. Place the shrimps in a zipper-lock plastic bag.

2. Add olive oil, chopped parsley, dry sherry, lemon zest, minced garlic, and salt in the plastic bag then shake to combine.

3. Marinate the shrimps for at least an hour and store in the refrigerator to keep the shrimps fresh.

4. Meanwhile, preheat the smoker to 225°F (107°C).

5. When the smoker has reached the desired temperature, transfer the shrimps to a disposable aluminum pan then place in the smoker.

6. Smoke the shrimps for 30 minutes.

7. Meanwhile, place all the sauce ingredients in a saucepan then stir well.

8. Bring to a simmer over medium heat then stir continuously until thickened.

9. Transfer to a sauce bowl then set aside.

10. Once the smoked shrimps are done, remove from the smoker then place on a serving dish.

11. Serve with the sauce.

12. Enjoy!

Smoked Crab Black Pepper

(TOTAL COOK TIME 30 MINUTES)

INGREDIENTS FOR 10 SERVINGS

- King Crab – 10 (5-lbs., 2.3-kgs)

THE SPICE

- Butter – 2 cups

- Smoked paprika – 3 tablespoons

- Black Pepper – 3 tablespoons

- Minced garlic – ¼ cup

- Lemon juice – ¼ cup

- Chopped parsley – ¼ cup

THE FIRE

- Preheat the smoker an hour prior to smoking.

- Add charcoal and hickory chips during the smoking time.

METHOD

1. Preheat a smoker to 225°F (107°C) and use indirect heat.

2. Place the crab in a disposable aluminum pan then add butter, smoked paprika, black pepper, minced garlic, lemon juice, and chopped parsley over the crab. Toss until just combined.

3. Once the smoker has reached the desired temperature, place the disposable aluminum pan in the smoker.

4. Smoke the crabs for 30 minutes.

5. When the crabs are done, take the pan out from the smoker then let it sit for a few minutes.

6. Transfer to a serving dish then serve right away.5

SIMPLE SMOKED MUSSELS WITH HAZELNUT FLAVOR

(TOTAL COOK TIME 30 MINUTES)

INGREDIENTS FOR 10 SERVINGS

- Fresh mussels without shells (4-lbs., 1.8-kgs)

THE RUB

- White wine – 1 cup

- Hazelnut oil – ¼ cup

THE FIRE

- Preheat the smoker an hour prior to smoking.

- Add alder wood chips during the smoking time.

METHOD

1. Preheat a smoker to 225°F (107°C).

2. Place the mussels in a disposable aluminum and spread evenly.

3. Pour white wine and hazelnut oil over the mussels.

4. Smoke the mussels for 30 minutes and once it is done, remove from the smoker and transfer to a serving dish.

5. Serve and enjoy immediately.

Lemon Smoked Lobster Tails Garlic

(TOTAL COOK TIME 50 MINUTES)

INGREDIENTS FOR 10 SERVINGS

- Lobster Tails – 10 (5-lbs., 2.3-kgs)

The Spice

- Lemon juice – ¾ cup

- Butter – 1 cup

- Smoked paprika – 1 ½ tablespoons

- Minced garlic – 2 tablespoons

- Old Bay Seasoning – 1 ½ tablespoons

- Salt – 1 ½ tablespoons

The Fire

- Preheat the smoker an hour prior to smoking.

- Add charcoal and hickory chips during the smoking time.

Method

1. Preheat the smoker to 225°F (107°C).

2. Melt butter in a saucepan then add smoked paprika, minced garlic, Old Bay seasoning, and salt to the saucepan.

3. Pour lemon juice into the saucepan then mix well. Remove from heat.

4. Cut the tough part of the lobster then brush with the seasoning mixture.

5. Place the lobsters on the smoker rack and smoke for 45 minutes. Brush the lobster with the seasoning mixture once every 10 minutes.

6. Smoke until the internal temperature has reached 140°F (60°C).

7. Once it is done, remove from the smoker then place on a serving dish.

8. Serve and enjoy.

SMOKED SWEET SHRIMPS WITH CARAWAY SEEDS

(TOTAL COOK TIME 30 MINUTES)

INGREDIENTS FOR 10 SERVINGS

- Fresh Shrimps (5-lbs., 2.3-kgs)

THE SPICE

- Sugar – 1 tablespoon

- Caraway seeds – 1 tablespoon

- Salt – 2 teaspoons

The Fire

- Preheat the smoker an hour prior to smoking.

- Use charcoal and hickory chips for smoking.

Method

1. Preheat the smoker to 225°F (107°C).

2. Peel the shrimps then place in a disposable aluminum pan.

3. Add sugar, salt, and caraway seeds to the pan then stir well.

4. Place the pan on the smoker rack then smoke the shrimps for 30 minutes.

5. When the shrimps are done, remove from the smoker then transfer to a serving dish.

6. Serve and enjoy.

Spiced Smoked Mussels with Garlic

(TOTAL COOK TIME 30 MINUTES)

INGREDIENTS FOR 10 SERVINGS

- Fresh mussels with shells (10-lbs., 4.5-kgs)

THE RUB

- Butter – 1 cup

- Olive oil – ¼ cup

- Minced garlic – 2 tablespoons

- Sliced shallots – 2 tablespoons

- Chopped parsley – ¼ cup

- White wine – 1 ½ cups

- Rosemary – 4 sprigs

- Thyme – 4 sprigs

THE FIRE

- Preheat the smoker an hour prior to smoking.

- Add pecan wood chips during the smoking time.

METHOD

1. Preheat a smoker to 225°F (107°C).

2. Wash and clean the mussels properly then set aside.

3. Melt the butter then combine with olive oil, minced garlic, sliced shallots, chopped parsley and white wine.

4. Rub the mussels with the spice mixture then place on a large sheet of aluminum foil. Divide into 3 or 4 batches if it is necessary.

5. Add rosemary and thyme to each batch of mussels then wrap with aluminum foil.

6. Place the wrapped mussels in the smoker then smoke the mussels for 30 minutes.

7. Once it is done, remove from the smoker and let them sit for a few minutes.

8. Unwrap the mussels and place on a serving dish.

9. Serve and enjoy.

INFORMATION ABOUT SMOKING MEAT

WHAT IS THE PRIMARY DIFFERENCE BETWEEN BARBECUING A MEAT AND SMOKING IT?

You might not believe it, but there are still people who think that the process of Barbecuing and Smoking are the same! So, this is something which you should know about before diving in deeper.

So, whenever you are going to use a traditional BBQ grill, you always put your meat directly on top of the heat source for a brief amount of time which eventually cooks up the meal. Smoking, on the other hand, will require you to combine the heat from your grill as well as the smoke to infuse a delicious smoky texture and flavor to your meat. Smoking usually takes much longer than traditional barbecuing. In most cases, it takes a minimum of 2 hours and a temperature of 100 -120 degrees for the smoke to be properly infused into the meat. Keep in mind that the time and temperature will obviously depend on the type of meat that you are using, and that is why it is suggested that you keep a meat thermometer handy to ensure that your meat is doing fine. Keep in mind that this method of barbecuing is also known as "Low and slow" smoking as well. With that cleared up, you should be aware that there are actually two different ways through which smoking is done.

THE CORE DIFFERENCE BETWEEN COLD AND HOT SMOKING

Depending on the type of grill that you are using, you might be able to get the option to go for a Hot Smoking Method or a Cold Smoking One. The primary fact about these three different cooking techniques which you should keep in mind are as follows:

- Hot Smoking: In this technique, the food will use both the heat on your grill and the smoke to prepare your food. This method is most suitable for items such as chicken, lamb, brisket etc.
- Cold Smoking: In this method, you are going to smoke your meat at a very low temperature such as 30 degree Celsius, making sure that it doesn't come into the direct contact with the heat. This is mostly used as a means to preserve meat and extend their life on the shelf.
- Roasting Smoke: This is also known as Smoke Baking. This process is essentially a combined form of both roasting and baking and can be performed in any type of smoker with a capacity of reaching temperatures above 82 degree Celsius.

THE DIFFERENT TYPES OF AVAILABLE SMOKERS

Essentially, what you should know is that right now in the market, you are going to get three different types of Smokers.

Charcoal Smoker

These types of smokers are hands down the best one for infusing the perfect Smoky flavor to your meat. But be warned, though, that these smokers are a little bit difficult to master as the method of regulating temperature is a little bit difficult when compared to normal Gas or Electric smokers.

Electric Smoker

After the charcoal smoker, next comes perhaps the simpler option, Electric Smokers. These are easy to use and plug and play type. All you need to do is just plug in, set the temperature and go about your daily life. The smoker will do the rest. However, keep in mind that the finishing smoky flavor won't be as intense as the Charcoal one.

Gas Smokers

Finally, comes the Gas Smokers. These have a fairly easy mechanism for temperature control and are powered usually by LP Gas. The drawback of these Smokers is that you are going to have to keep checking up on your Smoker every now and then to ensure that it has not run out of Gas.

THE DIFFERENT STYLES OF SMOKERS

The different styles of Smokers are essentially divided into the following.

Vertical (Bullet Style Using Charcoal)

These are usually low-cost solutions and are perfect for first-time smokers.

Vertical (Cabinet Style)

These Smokers come with a square shaped design with cabinets and drawers/trays for easy accessibility. These cookers also come with a water tray and a designated wood chips box as well.

Offset

These type of smokers have dedicated fireboxes that are attached to the side of the main grill. The smoke and heat required for these are generated from the firebox itself which is then passed through the main chamber and out through a nicely placed chimney.

Kamado Joe

And finally, we have the Kamado Joe which is ceramic smokers are largely regarded as being the "Jack Of All Trades".

These smokers can be used as low and slow smokers, grills, hi or low-temperature ovens and so on.

They have a very thick ceramic wall which allows it to hold heat better than any other type of smoker out there, requiring only a little amount of charcoal.

These are easy to use with better insulation and are more efficient when it comes to fuel control.

THE DIFFERENT TYPES OF WOOD AND THEIR BENEFITS

The Different Types Of Wood	Suitable For
Hickory	Wild game, chicken, pork, cheeses, beef
Pecan	Chicken, pork, lamb, cheeses, fish.
Mesquite	Beef and vegetables
Alder	Swordfish, Salmon, Sturgeon and other types of fishes. Works well with pork and chicken too.
Oak	Beef or briskets
Maple	Vegetable, ham or poultry
Cherry	Game birds, poultry or pork
Apple	Game birds, poultry, beef
Peach	Game birds, poultry or pork
Grape Vines	Beef, chicken or turkey
Wine Barrel Chips	Turkey, beef, chicken or cheeses
Seaweed	Lobster, mussels, crab, shrimp etc.
Herbs or Spices such as rosemary, bay leaves, mint,	Good for cheeses or vegetables and a small collection of light meats such as fillets or fish steaks.

lemon	**peels,**
whole	**nutmeg**
etc.	

But if you are one of that more "Daring" person out there and want to go ahead and try out the Charcoal cookers, then you are going to need to know about the different types of Charcoal as well.

THE DIFFERENT TYPES OF CHARCOAL

In General, there are essentially three different types of Charcoals. All of them are basically porous residues of black color that are made of carbon and ashes. However, the following are a little bit distinguishable due to their specific features.

- **BBQ Briquettes:** These are the ones that are made from a fine blend of charcoal and char.
- **Charcoal Briquettes:** These are created by compressing charcoal and are made from sawdust or wood products.
- **Lump Charcoal:** These are made directly from hardwood and are the most premium quality charcoals available. They are completely natural and are free from any form of the additive.

THE BASIC PREPARATIONS

- Always be prepared to spend the whole day and take as much time as possible to smoke your meat for maximum effect.
- Make sure to obtain the perfect Ribs/Meat for the meal which you are trying to smoke. Do a little bit of research if you need.
- I have already added a list of woods in this book, consult to that list and choose the perfect wood for your meal.
- Make sure to prepare the marinade for each of the meals properly. A great deal of the flavor comes from the rubbing.
- Keep a meat thermometer handy to get the internal temperature when needed.
- Use mittens or tongs to keep yourself safe
- Refrain yourself from using charcoal infused alongside starter fluid as it might bring a very unpleasant odor to your food
- Always make sure to start off with a small amount of wood and keep adding them as you cook.
- Don't be afraid to experiment with different types of wood for newer flavor and experiences.
- Always keep a notebook near you and note jot down whatever you are doing or learning and use them during the future session. This will help you to evolve and move forward.

THE CORE ELEMENTS OF SMOKING!

Smoking is a very indirect method of cooking that relies on a number of different factors to give you the most perfectly cooked meal that you are looking for. Each of these components is very important to the whole process as they all work together to create the meal of your dreams.

- **Time**: Unlike grilling or even Barbequing, smoking takes a really long time and requires a whole lot of patience. It takes time for the smoky flavor to slowly get infused into the meats. Jus to bring things into comparison, it takes an about 8 minutes to fully cook a steak through direct heating, while smoking (indirect heating) will take around 35-40 minutes.

- **Temperature:** When it comes to smoking, the temperature is affected by a lot of different factors that are not only limited to the wind, cold air temperatures but also the cooking wood's dryness. Some smokers work best with large fires that are controlled by the draw of a chimney and restricted airflow through the various vents of the cooking chamber and firebox. While other smokers tend to require smaller fire with fewer coals as well as a completely different combination of the vent and draw controls. However, most smokers are designed to work at temperatures as low as 180 degrees Fahrenheit to as high as 300 degrees Fahrenheit. But the recommend temperature usually falls between 250 degrees Fahrenheit and 275 degrees Fahrenheit.

- **Airflow:** The level of air to which the fire is exposed to greatly determines how your fire will burn and how quickly it will burn the fuel. For instance, if you restrict air flow into the firebox by closing up the available vents, then the fire will burn at a low temperature and vice versa. Typically in smokers, after lighting up the fire, the vents are opened to allow for maximum air flow and is then adjusted throughout the cooking process to make sure that optimum flame is achieved.
- **Insulation:** Insulation is also very important when it comes to smokers as it helps to easily manage the cooking process throughout the whole cooking session. A good insulation allows smokers to efficiently reach the desired temperature instead of waiting for hours upon hours!

Get Your FREE Gift

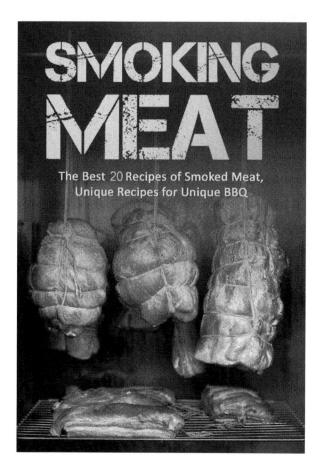

Suscribe to our Mail List and get your FREE copy of the book

'Smoking Meat: The Best 20 Recipes of Smoked Meat, Unique Recipes for Unique BBQ'

http://tiny.cc/smoke20

CONCLUSION

I can't express how honored I am to think that you found my book interesting and informative enough to read it all through to the end. I thank you again for purchasing this book and I hope that you had as much fun reading it as I had writing it. I bid you farewell and encourage you to move forward and find your true Smoked Fish spirit!

OTHER BOOKS BY ADAM JONES

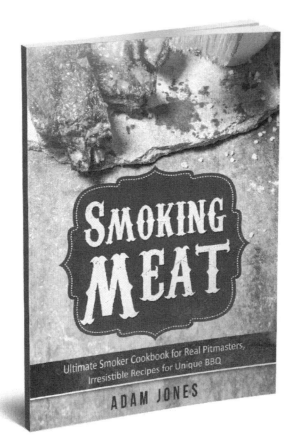

https://www.amazon.com/dp/B07B3R82P4

https://www.amazon.com/dp/1548040959

https://www.amazon.com/dp/1979559902

https://www.amazon.com/dp/1544791178

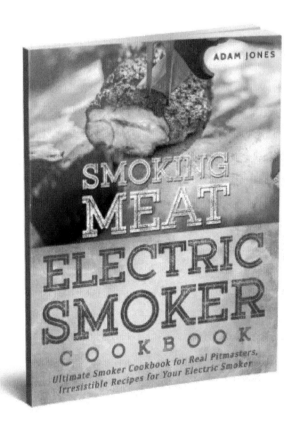

https://www.amazon.com/dp/1979811318

https://www.amazon.com/dp/1546605916

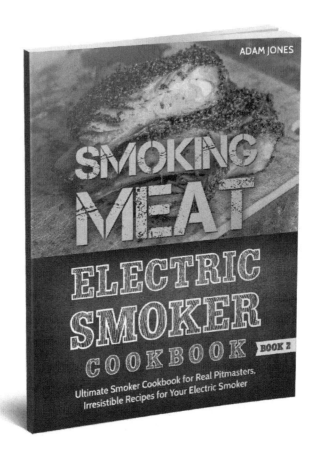

https://www.amazon.com/dp/1981617973

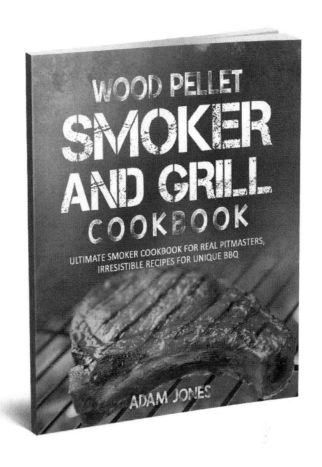

https://www.amazon.com/dp/1981940693

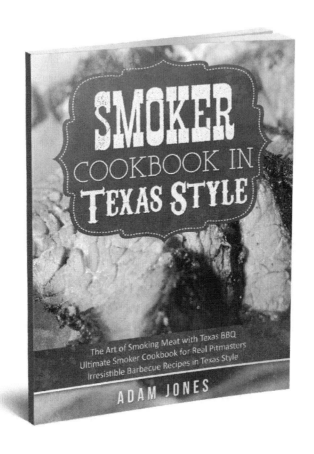

https://www.amazon.com/dp/B07B4YDKJ5

https://www.amazon.com/dp/1977677347

https://www.amazon.com/dp/1542597846

https://www.amazon.com/dp/154418199X

P.S. Thank you for reading this book. If you've enjoyed this book, please don't shy, drop me a line, leave a feedback or both on Amazon. I love reading feedbacks and your opinion is extremely important for me.

My Amazon page:
www.amazon.com/author/adjones

ISBN-13: 978-1987566055

ISBN-10: 198756605X

Made in the USA
San Bernardino, CA
03 May 2019